THE HOUSEHOLD TREASURY:
Harvester Edition

STARTER KIT– A SIMPLE MONEY STRUCTURE FOR WORKING PEOPLE

BY K.M.W.

The Household Treasury Series

I. Harvester Edition (Starter Kit for Working Incomes)

II. Evergreen Edition (Standard Volume): Forthcoming

III. Cellar Red Edition (Advanced Volume/ Limited): Forthcoming

For permission requests, contact:

Household Treasury Press

householdtreasurypress@gmail.com

Title: The Household Treasury: Harvester Edition– Starter Kit

Author: K.M.W.

First Edition: 2026

Published by Household Treasury Press

Dallas, Texas

Print ISBN: 979-8-9944166-0-0

DISCLAIMER

Contents

PREFACE — WHY THIS EXISTS

Most money advice you've seen wasn't written for you.

It was written for one of three audiences:

> people who already have money,
>
> people selling you a lifestyle, or
>
> people who get paid to keep you confused.

If you earn a working income, pay real bills, and feel like you should be further along by now, most of what's out there either talks down to you or talks past you.

> You don't need to "manifest abundance."
>
> You don't need to "budget harder."
>
> You don't need a vision board or a side hustle or a five-year plan on a whiteboard.
>
> You need a **structure**.

You need a way to *tell every* paycheck:

> where it goes,
>
> what its job is, and
>
> what happens when life punches you in the mouth.

That's it.

The Harvester Edition starter kit is not about becoming rich in 90 days. It's not about pretending the game is fair.

It's about turning your household into a small, stubborn treasury:

> your **bills** still get paid,
>
> your **Moat** slowly thickens,
>
> your **money** starts to pay you back,
>
> and your **future** stops depending on whether you have a "good month" or not.

You don't have to be perfect to use this.

You just have to be willing to:

> give your money defined jobs,
>
> follow one routing rule most of the time,
>
> and not panic when things go sideways.

If you can do that, this little structure will quietly start repairing things the world told you were permanent.

The rest of this book is just instructions.

— **K.M.W.**

THE HOUSEHOLD TREASURY AT A GLANCE…

What this is

A simple structure that tells every paycheck:

where to go,

what its job is,

and what to do when life hits you in the mouth.

Not a budget. A small, stubborn treasury for your household.

The three rules

1. Routing Rule – A fixed slice of every paycheck goes to the Treasury first. Life runs on the rest.

2. Job Rule – Money has different jobs:
    keeping today alive,
    thickening your Moat,
    paying you back (Ladder)
    and funding the Long Run.

3. Chain of Command – When money must come out, you pull it in this order:

Pool → Moat → Ladder → Long Run (last).

For the next few months:

pick a percentage you can actually hit (10–33%),

let that slice leave your Life account every time you're paid,

track Moat thickness in months of expenses,

and follow the chain of command when something breaks.

If money feels even slightly less chaotic after a few months, the system is working.

The rest of this book just explains how to build it and live with it.

CHAPTER 1

YOUR MONEY ISN'T LAZY,
IT'S UNEMPLOYED

If you're reading this, I'm going to assume three things:

1. You work.

2. The money shows up.

3. The money disappears.

On paper, you "know" where it goes:

- rent or mortgage
- food
- gas or transit
- phone, internet, utilities
- subscriptions, random runs to the store
- whatever's left, which usually isn't much

People will tell you, "your money is lazy" or "you're bad with money."

That's not what's happening.

Your money isn't lazy. **It's unemployed.**

No one ever showed you how to put it to work, so it wanders: a little to bills, a little to panic, a little to "I'll figure it out later."

With no job description and no chain of command, it just gets dragged into whatever problem is screaming the loudest that week.

Rent is yelling. Groceries are yelling. The car is coughing. The card payment is lurking. Something fun is begging for attention because life has been heavy.

There's no structure, so of course it feels chaotic.

You don't fix chaos by yelling "budget harder."

You fix chaos by giving every dollar a **role** and a **route**:

This money pays for **Life.**

This money thickens the **Moat.**

This money feeds the **Ladder.**

This money is for the **Long Run**.

<table>
<tr><td>Life
Bills, food,
transport, basics.</td><td>Moat
Safety buffer
measured in weeks.</td></tr>
<tr><td>Ladder
Short-term, safe
pieces that pay you back.</td><td>Long Run
Slow compounding
and future freedom.</td></tr>
</table>

Figure 1 – The four jobs your money can have.

That's a household treasury.

This book will show you how to build one that works on a working income.

No fantasy salary required.

CHAPTER 2

WHAT A HOUSEHOLD TREASURY ACTUALLY IS

Governments have treasuries. Corporations have treasuries.

You should too.

A **treasury** is not just "a pile of money."

It's a **set of rules** about:

what money is for,

where it sits,

when it can move, and

who is allowed to touch it.

Your household treasury has four main **jobs** for your money. Don't worry about the names yet; focus on the logic.

1. Life — keeping today alive

This is the money that pays for:

rent or mortgage

utilities, phone, internet

groceries, gas, basic transport

minimum payments you actually owe

basic personal care

Life money keeps you alive **this month**. It doesn't have to be fancy, just honest.

2. Moat — making one problem survivable

This is your **safety buffer**:

emergency cash

short-term savings for known hits (like annual car insurance)

the difference between "annoying problem" and "my whole life fell apart"

This is not "savings for something fun."

This is the money that keeps a single event from ruining the whole year.

3. Ladder — money that pays you back

This is the boring part of your treasury that quietly **earns**:

safe yield from things like T-Bills or cash-like funds

interest from solid, low-risk instruments

maybe, over time, slices of reliable dividend-paying investments

This is not the crypto lottery. This is not day trading.

This is the part of your world where **money works** so you don't have to work for every dollar forever.

4. Long Run — future you's territory

This is the part that lives on longer horizons:

broad stock index funds

long-term retirement accounts

patient ownership of real businesses through the market

This is the money that future you will thank you for even if current you grumbles about it.

How They Fit Together

Here's the core idea:

Life keeps you functioning.

Moat protects Life from getting wrecked.

Ladder takes pressure off Life over time.

Long Run is how you stop being fragile when you're older.

You don't need fancy products to start.

You just need:

- a checking account for your **Life**,
- a savings-type account for your **Moat** (*the Evergreen Edition* covers Moat vehicle options in more detail).
- a basic brokerage or similar account for your **Ladder** and **Long Run**.

The rest is about routing money into the right places in the right order.

That's what we do next.

A quick way to picture this: the company's math ends where yours begins.

At work, the equation is basically:

Revenue – Costs – Everything Else = Your Paycheck.

Your Household Treasury flips the frame:

1. **Add** – Your paycheck lands.

2. **Divide** – Your routing rule slices it for Treasury vs Life.

3. **Multiply** – Moat and Ladder earn simple yield over time.

4. **Exponents** – Compounding shows up when you let that yield stack instead of raiding it.

5. **Parentheses** – Later, accounts and entities just sit around this flow like brackets, protecting and directing it.

The big shift is simple: payroll is the company's end of the math and your beginning.

CHAPTER 3

SETTING UP YOUR TREASURY IN A WEEKEND

In this structure, 'Treasury' means everything outside of **Life** (Moat + Ladder + Long Run), whether you hold it in one account or several.

Step 1 — Name What You Already Have and Add What You Need

Most people have:

- one checking account
- one savings account
- a brokerage account- Note: for efficiency this type of account can serve all purposes of your Household Treasury
- maybe a retirement account through work (likely a 401k)

If you don't have a brokerage or retirement account at all, you're not behind—you just know what to open next.

You're going to **rename them in your head** before you touch anything in the bank app.

- Main checking → **Life**
- Savings / high-yield savings → **Moat**
- Brokerage / retirement / investment account → **Treasury Account**
  Internally, you will later split this into Ladder and Long Run.

Step 2 — Make Space for the Treasury Flow

Your paycheck currently:

- hits checking,
- gets eaten by Life.

You want:

- Paycheck → **Treasury slice** goes out,
- remainder stays for **Life**.

You can do this one of two ways:

1. **Split at the employer level**

   Many employers let you send your direct deposit to more than one account.

   You can set:

   > X% or fixed amount → Treasury Account
   > remainder → Life checking

   This is the cleanest version.

2. **Split using an automatic transfer**

   If your employer only hits one account, you can:

   > schedule an automatic transfer from Life checking → Treasury Account
   > on payday or the day after, for your chosen percentage or dollar amount.

Either way, the principle is:

"As close to paycheck as possible, the Treasury gets paid."

You're turning your Treasury into a "bill" that gets paid before the rest of your life gets noisy.

Step 3 — Start With a Simple Split of Your Treasury Flow

When money hits the Treasury, you don't need a complex allocation right away.

Here's a starter breakdown you can adjust later:

> **Half** goes to Moat (high-yield savings / cash-like fund).

> **Half** goes into the Treasury Account (brokerage / retirement) for investing.

Inside the Treasury Account:

Early on, you might just let it collect in a **cash-like fund** or settle in cash.

Once balances are meaningful, you can decide:

what portion becomes the **Ladder** (safe yield), and
what portion becomes **Long Run** (broad, long-term investments).

If you don't know which investment options to choose yet, that's okay.

The important thing at this stage:

the money is leaving Life,

hitting the Treasury Account,

and staying there.

You can refine the mix later. You cannot refine money that never made it out of checking.

Step 4 — Make a One-Page Map for Yourself

Grab an index card or a half sheet of paper and write:

Life — [Bank name] Checking, ending in _________

Moat — [Bank name] Savings, ending in _________

Treasury — [Broker / plan] account, ending in _______

– Ladder lives here

– Long Run lives here

Somewhere on that same piece of paper:

Routing rule: ______% of every paycheck goes to the Treasury.

Life runs on the rest.

Put this where you actually see it: in your wallet, by your desk, taped to the refrigerator, whatever.

This is your **personal operating diagram.**

You now have:

named accounts,

a routing rule,

and a place to send the money.

The Point Isn't Perfection

There will be months you don't hit the exact percentage.

You're human.

The point is that **there is a number** and **you aim at it on purpose**. When you miss, you treat it as a deviation, not "oh well, that's just how it goes."

The routing rule is the spine of the Household Treasury.

If this is all you did—picked a realistic percentage and sent it into your Treasury before Life—you'd be ahead of most people.

The next chapter makes that routing possible without needing a spreadsheet or a finance degree.

CHAPTER 4

THE ROUTING RULE

Most people run this silent rule:

"Bills first. Chaos second. Hope there's something left to save."

Your treasury flips that.

You're going to use one simple **routing rule**:

A fixed slice of every paycheck goes to the treasury first. Life runs on the rest.

That slice doesn't have to be huge on day one. What matters is:

it happens **first**,

it's the same **percentage**,

and you treat it like a non-negotiable bill you pay to yourself.

A common starter number is **33% of take-home pay**.

Not because 33 is magic, but because:

it's big enough to matter,

small enough that Life still has space,

and it forces you to confront what you're doing with the 67%.

If 33% is impossible right now, you start lower.

Maybe 20%.

Maybe 15%.

Whatever the number, the rule is the same:

Treasury, then Life.

Not Life, then "maybe some leftovers."

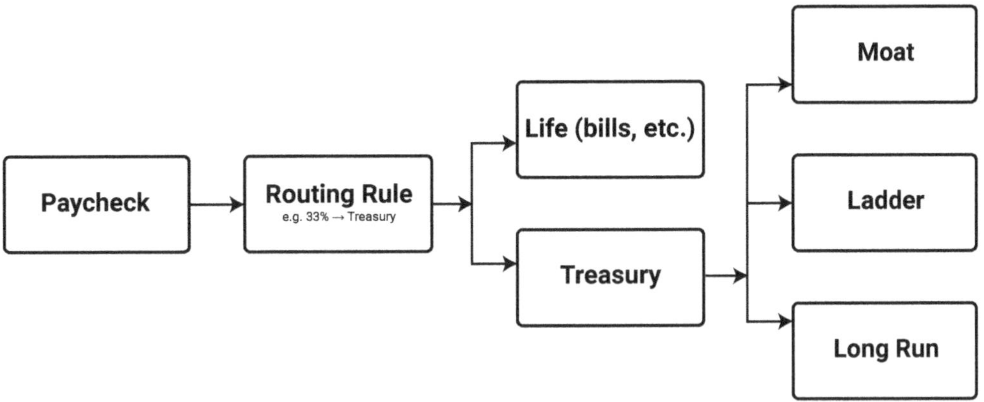

Figure 2 – One Routing Rule applied to every paycheck.

Quick Examples (Numbers That Actually Feel Like Your Paychecks)

Let's say:

you bring home **$2,400/month** (roughly $600/week).

Example 1 — 33% routing

$2,400 × 33% ≈ **$800 to the Treasury**

$1,600 left for Life

Inside that $800, you'd later divide between:

Moat

Ladder

Long Run

...but we don't have to slice it yet. For now, we're just proving we can **reserve** the $800.

Example 2 — 20% routing

If 33% makes Life impossible for now:

$2,400 × 20% = **$480 to the Treasury**

$1,920 left for Life

It's less aggressive, but it's still a real number. It's still a routing rule, not "whatever's left."

CHAPTER 4A

A WORKED EXAMPLE (REAL NUMBERS)

Let's make this concrete.

We'll walk through a single person:

Take-home income: $2,400/month (roughly $600/week)

Current situation:

no savings,
random card balances,
always one bill behind,
no investments

We'll compare what they're doing now to what happens under the Household Treasury over 3 months.

Before the Treasury

Right now, their month looks something like this:

Rent: $900

Utilities + phone + internet: $250

Groceries: $400

Gas / transport: $150

Minimum payments: $200

Everything else: $700 disappears into "I don't even know"

No defined roles. No routing rule. No Moat.

One car repair or missed shift and something doesn't get paid.

Step 1 — Install a 25% routing rule

Instead of aiming straight at 33%, they start with:

25% of every paycheck goes to the Treasury. Life runs on the other 75%.

On $2,400/month:

25% = $600 to the Treasury

$1,800 left for Life

That means:

Life has to live on $1,800 instead of $2,400.

The extra $600 is no longer allowed to disappear.

Step 2 — Split the Treasury money simply

For the first three months, they use a simple split:

60% of Treasury flow → Moat

40% of Treasury flow → Treasury Account (Ladder + Long Run)

On $600/month:

Moat: $360/month

Treasury Account: $240/month

Month 1 — Nothing fancy, just flow

At the end of Month 1:

Moat: $360

Treasury Account: $240

Total Treasury: $600

Life feels tighter, but not impossible:

They cut $100 of pure nonsense out of the $700 "I don't even know" category.

They push one non-urgent purchase into "later."

Nothing magic happened.

What matters is: for the first time, $600 didn't vanish.

Month 2 — The first hit

Month 2, something breaks:

$350 car repair.

Chain of command:

1. Pool has $100 spare in checking.

2. Moat has $360 from last month.

They do:

$100 from Pool

$250 from Moat

Moat drops from $360 → $110.

Treasury flow for Month 2 is still:

$600 in

60% ($360) to Moat

40% ($240) to Treasury Account

End of Month 2 balances:

Moat: $110 + $360 = $470

Treasury Account: previous $240 + new $240 = $480

Total Treasury: $950

If they had no structure, that entire $350 would have landed on a card or bounced something else.

Instead, the system took the hit the way it was designed to.

Month 3 — Moat thickens

No major hits this month.

They keep the same:

income ($2,400),

routing (25%),

internal split (60/40).

Treasury flow:

another $360 to Moat

another $240 to Treasury Account

End of Month 3:

Moat: $470 + $360 = $830

Treasury Account: $480 + $240 = $720

Total Treasury: $1,550

Moat thickness:

Assume Life spending has settled around $1,700/month now (they've learned to survive without random leaks).

$830 ÷ $1,700 ≈ 0.49 months of Moat, call it two weeks of full expenses.

Three months ago, they had zero.

Now the car repair didn't wreck them, and they have:

half a month of runway,

$720 in a Treasury Account that's ready to be shaped into Ladder + Long Run.

All of that came from one decision:

"25% of my take-home goes to the Treasury before Life sees it."

No side hustle. No miracle. No spreadsheets.

Surplus & Deficit Resolution

If Life expenses are less than *Life inflow*, the remainder is a **Surplus** and is routed according to the allocation rules:

Moat → Ladder→ Long Run

If Life expenses are greater than Life inflow, the difference is a **Deficit** and must be covered by reversing the stack in order:

Pool, then Moat, then Ladder (only if necessary)

Life still goes to zero each month after bills; the Treasury balances shown are what remains outside of life.

The next chapter is how to live with it month after month without burning out.

CHAPTER 5

HOW TO RUN IT MONTH AFTER MONTH

You don't need daily rituals. You need two small habits:

a **payday ritual**, and

a **once-a-month check-in**.

Payday Ritual (10–15 minutes)

Whenever money hits:

1. Confirm that the **Treasury transfer** happened:

   Did the correct amount land in the Treasury Account?
   If you're still doing it manually, send it now.

2. Check that **Life** still has enough to cover:

   bills due before next payday,
   basic groceries and transport.

3. If Life is short:

   First, look for expenses to shift or cut.
   If there's truly no space, you can **lower the next transfer**, but do it
   consciously and write it down.

   That's it. No line-by-line budget.

Monthly Check-In (20–30 minutes)

Once a month, sit down and look at four things:

1. **Moat thickness**

   How much is in Moat (savings / buffer)?

   Divide that number by your average monthly Life spending.

   That's your **month(s) of runway**.

   Example: $1,800 in Moat / $900 monthly Life = 2 months.

2. **Treasury growth**

> How much total sits in the Treasury Account?
>
> Is it larger than last month?
>
> Did any income (dividends, interest) show up?

3. **Contribution accuracy**

> Over the last month, how many times did you hit your routing rule?
>
> 4 paychecks → 4 attempts.
>
> If you hit 3 out of 4, that's 75%. You're not failing, you're **measuring**.

4. **Stress level**

> Did money feel **slightly less chaotic** than the month before?
>
> Fewer overdrafts?
>
> Fewer "I have no idea where it all went" moments?

Write these on one sheet each month. You're building a little log of progress that doesn't live in your head.

Small Adjustments, Not Overhauls

If you're constantly short in Life:

> the routing percentage might be too aggressive **for now**, or
>
> Life spending is leaking in places you can realistically patch.

You adjust one notch at a time:

> 33% → 25% for a quarter (3 Months), or
>
> same % but you attack a specific expense cluster.
>
> The structure doesn't change. Just the size of the flow.
>
> Now the fun part: what happens when life hits you in the mouth.

CHAPTER 6

THE ANTI-PANIC PLAN: WHEN LIFE HITS YOU

At some point, something will happen:

> the car dies,
>
> hours get cut,
>
> someone gets sick,
>
> two big bills land at once.

This is where most people wipe out years of progress in one weekend.

You are going to follow **a chain of command** instead.

The Chain of Command

When money has to come **out**:

Pool → Moat → Ladder → Long Run
in that order.

Pool is whatever liquid cash is immediately at hand:

> cash in checking that's not bill-committed,
>
> tiny buffer inside Moat earmarked for "annoying but expected" issues.

If Pool isn't enough, you go up the stack.

You do **not**:

> start selling long-term investments first, or
>
> empty the Treasury because you're scared.

You follow the order.

Scenario 1 — The $600 Problem

Say:

> The car repair comes in at $600.
>
> Pool has $250.
>
> Moat has $900.
>
> Treasury Account has a growing balance.

Chain of command says:

1. $250 from Pool

2. $350 from Moat

3. Nothing from Ladder or Long Run

Then you write one short line in your monthly log:

"Car repair: drew $350 from Moat. Goal: refill Moat by $350 over next X months."

You haven't nuked the system. You've **used** it.

Scenario 2 — Short Paycheck Month

Hours got cut. Paycheck is down.

First, **protect the routing rule if possible**, even at a temporarily lower percentage.

Second, **trim Life** where you honestly can.

Third, if there's still a gap, use:

1. Pool

2. Moat

You only touch the Ladder or Long Run if:

it's a deep, sustained hit, and

you've exhausted sane options in Life and the Moat.

If you get to that point, you're no longer in "panic." You're in **controlled damage mode**, which leads into the next chapter.

CHAPTER 7

BEFORE YOU QUIT OR
LIQUIDATE

This is the chapter you read on the day you're ready to say:

"Screw this. I'm done. I'll just cash everything out."

You are allowed to be tired. You are allowed to pause.

You are **not** allowed to casually blow up your future.

1. Drop the Rate, Don't Drop the System

The first move is **not** "stop everything."

The first move is:

"I'm lowering my routing percentage for now, but I'm keeping the structure."

33% → 20%

20% → 10%

Write it down:

"For the next 3 months, routing rate = ______%. Revisit on [date]."

You keep:

Life account,

Moat account,

Treasury account,

Chain of command.

You're just letting the system breathe.

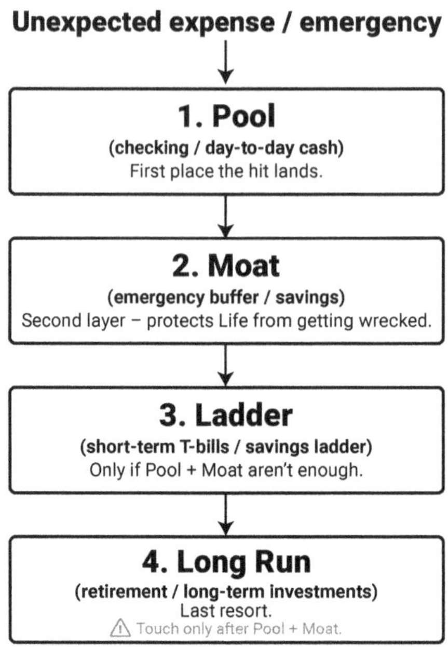

Figure 3 – Chain of Command When Life Hits You

2. Use the Chain of Command On Purpose

If you're facing a specific hit:

> follow Pool → Moat → Ladder → Long Run.

This might still hurt. You might still draw down Moat or even sell something.

The difference is **order and intent**, not emotion.

3. Don't Turn Taxes Into a Second Emergency

If you're thinking about:

> selling investments in taxable accounts, or
>
> touching retirement accounts,

pause and acknowledge:

> there may be **capital gains or losses**,
>
> there may be **penalties and extra tax**,
>
> the timing (mid-year vs year-end) may matter.

The next steps are:

1. Write down **exactly which account(s)** you're considering tapping.

2. Write down approximate **balances** and how much you're thinking of taking.

3. Talk to a **tax professional or planner** and ask:

   "What happens if I do this this year?"

   Even a modest one-time fee is cheaper than a surprise tax bill created because panic was in charge of your emergency decisions.

4. How to Unwind Like an Adult

If your reality is:

   long-term job loss,

   serious health event,

   major family crisis,

   you may need to unwind more than you'd like.

Do it in order:

1. **Freeze lifestyle creep.**

   No new subscriptions. No new fixed commitments.

2. **Turn off or shrink contributions.**

   Make it explicit: "Routing paused" or "Routing at 5% until further notice."

3. **Liquidate in chain order:**

   Pool → zero if needed
   Moat → down to a minimum floor you set
   Ladder → only as much as math truly demands
   Long Run → last resort, and preferably with professional input

4. **Do not close the accounts.**

   Empty is fine. Gone is not.
   You want the architecture to remain for when you can rebuild.

5. **Document the event.**

   One page:

   what you sold or drew down,
   why you did it,
   what "rebuild" will mean when you're ready.

   Future you shouldn't have to guess what happened.

5. Define "Back Online" Before You Need It

Before things go bad—or now, while you're calm—decide:

   "I will consider myself 'back online' when:
   – my bills are current again
   – I have at least one month of the Moat rebuilt
   – I can restart routing at _____%"

That blank is your number.

Having that target prevents you from drifting for years in "I'll restart someday" mode.

6. The Only Real Failure

Failure is not:

   lowering your rate,

   using the Moat,

   pausing contributions,

   unwinding in an orderly way under real pressure.

Failure is:

rage-selling everything,

flattening your future to zero,

and blaming it all on "the system" instead of your own panic.

This structure is here to **protect you from your worst money day**, not just your best intentions.

If you're reading this chapter, you're already taking it more seriously than most people ever will.

That counts.

CHAPTER 8

YOUR FIRST RUN AND
WHAT COMES AFTER

There's no magic number of days that makes this "work," but it helps to think in **runs** instead of forever.

Your first run is simple.

Month 1 — Build and Prove

Goals:

set up the accounts and names,

get the routing rule working at any realistic percentage,

survive one month without tearing the structure down.

Questions to ask yourself at the end of Month 1:

Did I route anything at all into the Treasury every time I was paid?

Do I know, in plain language, where my Moat lives and how big it is?

Did I avoid blind chaos transfers (moving money around without knowing why)?

If the answer is "yes" more often than "no," Month 1 did its job.

Month 2 — Thicken the Moat

Goals:

keep routing, even if you have to adjust the percentage,

make the **Moat thickness** a monthly number you track,

avoid new fixed expenses.

You want to see:

the Moat number climb, even slowly,

your stress level about "one surprise bill" comes down a notch.

Month 3 — Stabilize and Decide

Goals:

log three months of:

routing attempts,
Moat thickness,
Treasury balance,
and honest notes about how it felt.

At the end of Month 3, ask:

1. Is money **slightly less chaotic** than when I started?
2. Do I feel more or less fragile than I did before?
3. Can I explain my own system to someone else in under five minutes?

If the answers are mostly "more stable, less fragile, yes I can explain it," then:

The Household Treasury is installed.

You're out of "experiment" mode and into "this is how I run my money now."

From here, progression is simple:

gradually move more of the Treasury into the Ladder and Long Run positions,

keep thickening the Moat to your personal comfort level,

treat future raises and windfalls as **injections** into the Treasury instead of automatic lifestyle upgrades.

This is where the Household Treasury: Harvester Edition hands off to deeper work:

more detailed math,

more precise allocations,

and eventually the institutional, multi-entity side for people who need it.

But you don't need any of that to let this first version change your life.

You just need to keep running the simple version you've already built.

APPENDIX

APPENDIX A — Routing Calculator (Worksheet)

1. Monthly take-home income (after tax)

   $ ______________

2. Choose your starting routing percentage

   (Be honest. You can raise it later.)

   ☐ 10%   ☐ 15%   ☐ 20%   ☐ 25%   ☐ 33%   ☐ Other: _____%

3. Monthly Treasury amount

   Monthly income × routing % = $ ______________

4. Per-paycheck Treasury amount

   If you're paid:

   > Weekly: Treasury ÷ 4 = $ ______________
   > Every 2 weeks: Treasury ÷ 2 = $ ______________
   > Twice a month: Treasury ÷ 2 = $ ______________

5. Simple internal split for your first run

   ☐ 60% Moat / 40% Treasury Account

   ☐ 50% Moat / 50% Treasury Account

   ☐ Other: ______________ / ______________

6. Your written routing rule

"I route _____ % of every paycheck—about $ __________ , into my Household

Treasury: $__________ to Moat, $ ______________ to the Treasury Account."

APPENDIX B — Monthly Check-In Sheet

Month / Year: _______________________

1. Moat thickness

> Moat balance: $ _______________
> Average monthly Life spending: $ _______________
> Moat ÷ Life = _________ months of runway

2. Treasury Account

> Balance last month: $ _______________
> Balance this month: $ _______________
> Difference: $ _______________ (up / down)
> Any income (dividends / interest) you noticed: $ _______________

3. Routing accuracy

> Paychecks received: _________
> Times you hit your routing rule: _________
> Hit rate: _________ / _________ ≈ _________%

4. Stress check (circle one)

> This month felt:

☐ much worse ☐ worse ☐ about the same ☐ better ☐ much better

5. Notes

> "What helped: ____"
> "What hurt: ____"
> "One change to try next month: _________________________________"

APPENDIX C — Anti-Panic Card (*Copy This Somewhere You'll See It*)

When something breaks or a bill blindsides you:

1. **Pause.** No instant app transfers. No late-night selling.

2. **Chain of command for money coming out:**

3. Pool → Moat → Ladder → Long Run (last)

4. **If you're thinking about selling investments or touching retirement:**

    Write down **which account(s)** and **how much**.
    Contact a tax professional and ask:
    "What happens if I do this this year?"

5. **If you need to pause the system:**

    Lower the routing rate instead of deleting it.
    Don't close accounts. Empty is allowed; gone is not.
    Define your "back online" conditions and write them down.

You are allowed to be tired.

You are not allowed to casually burn down your future.

APPENDIX D — "Back Online" Definition

Very simple template:

My "Back Online" Conditions

I will consider myself "back online" when:

My bills are current again.

My Moat balance is at least $____________ (about _______ months of Life).

I can restart routing at _____% of my take-home.

Optional:

I have rebuilt the amount I had to draw from Moat / Treasury: $____________

Signed: ______________________________

Date: ______________________________

APPENDIX E — Quick FAQ

Q: I have debt. Shouldn't I just attack that first?

A: If a debt is actively burning your life down (legal threats, collections, predatory interest), it goes in the "Life and safety first" category. This Starter Kit doesn't say "ignore debt." It says "don't stay structurally naked forever." You can run a smaller routing percentage while you attack the worst debts, but keeping **some** flow into your Treasury is how you stop having to rebuild from zero every time.

Q: My income is irregular. How do I use a routing rule?

A: Pick a **percentage**, not a dollar amount. Every time you get paid—hourly, gig, tips, whatever—you skim that percentage into the Treasury. On big weeks, more flows in. On small weeks, less, but the rule is the same. Your monthly check-in will show you the average.

Q: What if my partner doesn't want to do this?

A: You can still run a Household Treasury on **your side of the income**. You can share Life expenses and quietly build Moat, Ladder, and Long Run with your portion. If it works, results speak louder than arguments.

Q: Is this going to make me rich?

A: This is going to make you **less fragile and less random**. That's the point. Wealth comes from time, income, and choices. This structure makes better use of whatever you have, whether that's $2,000/month or $20,000/month.

APPENDIX F — HOUSEHOLD TREASURY LANGUAGE (Quick Reference)

You can treat this page as your "pronunciation guide" for the whole system.

The Three Core Rules

Routing Rule – A fixed slice of every paycheck goes to the Household Treasury first. Life runs on what's left. In the Harvester Edition, the Phase 1 target floor is 33% of take-home.

Job Rule – Money does different jobs:

keeping today alive (**Life**),
thickening your safety buffer (**Moat**),
paying you back (**Ladder**)
funding the **Long Run**

Chain of Command – When money has to come out, it leaves in this order:

Pool → Moat → Ladder → Long Run (last)

If you follow the Routing Rule on the way in and the Chain of Command on the way out, the structure does most of the thinking for you.

Key Metrics

Moat Thickness – Moat balance ÷ bare-bones monthly Life spending = months of runway.

Treasury Flow Rate – The percentage of take-home currently routing into the Household Treasury (your 10–33%+).

Contribution Floor – The minimum routing rate you refuse to drop below unless it's a true emergency.

Order of Work (one-line version) – Company math ends with your paycheck. Household Treasury math starts with it:

Add income → Divide by your routing rule → Let Moat and Ladder Multiply → Long Run Compounds exponentially → Life spends what's left.

AFTERWORD — YOU DON'T HAVE TO IMPRESS ANYONE

If you've made it this far, you've done something most people never will:

you looked at your money with clear eyes,

you admitted that "hope and vibes" aren't a structure,

and you bothered to install a new way of doing things.

No one is going to throw you a parade for that.

There won't be a confetti cannon when your Moat hits three months, or when your Treasury quietly crosses a number that used to feel impossible.

Most of the wins in this system are **invisible**:

the crisis that didn't wreck your year,

the overdraft that never happened,

the night you slept instead of spiraling about bills,

the future tax bill that never got created because you didn't panic-sell everything.

You won't be able to post those. That's fine.

This structure is not for the internet. It's for you, the people under your roof, and the version of you who has to live with the long-term consequences of today's choices.

You don't have to impress anyone.

You don't have to turn this into a personality.

You just have to keep:

giving your money jobs,

following the routing rule most of the time,

and respecting the chain of command when life gets loud.

If you do that, month after month, this "little" Household Treasury will quietly turn into one of the most important things you ever built.

And if you fall off for a while?

You already know how to pause without destroying it, how to come back without shame, and how to keep future-you in the room when present-you is tired.

That's more than most people ever get.

Stay steady. Re-route the next paycheck. Thickening the Moat counts as a win every single time.

— **K.M.W.**

NEXT LAYERS
(FOR WHEN YOU'RE READY)

If you've run the Harvester Edition starter kit for a while and you:

knew your routing rule by heart,

can quote your Moat thickness without checking your banking app,

and have watched your Treasury survive at least one real-life punch,

then you're ready for deeper layers:

turning more of the Treasury into a real income engine,

shaping the Long Run around your actual life timeline,

and, for some people, learning how to use this framework at the level of businesses, trusts, and serious wealth.

Those are separate books.

This one had one job:
give your money a basic chain of command and stop you from blowing yourself up in the meantime.

If it did that, even a little, you've already changed your trajectory.